GREGORY L. VOGT

SATURN

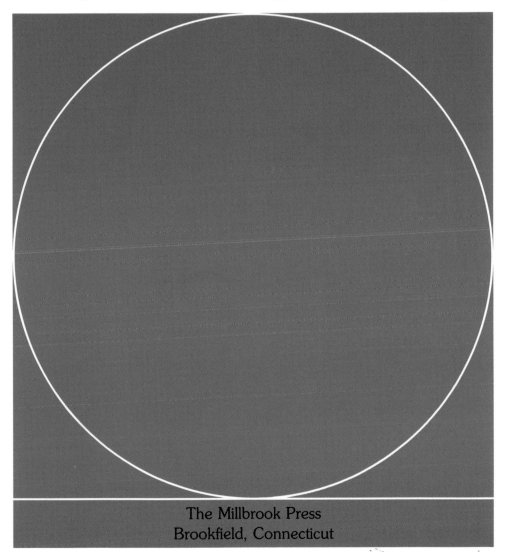

The Millbrook Press
Brookfield, Connecticut

viva

Published by The Millbrook Press
2 Old New Milford Road
Brookfield, Connecticut 06804

Library of Congress Cataloging-in-Publication Data

Vogt, Gregory.
Saturn / Gregory L. Vogt.
p.   cm.—(Gateway solar system)
Includes bibliographical references and index.
Summary: Presents information known about Saturn, its
rings, and moons.
ISBN 1-56294-332-4 (lib. bdg.)
1. Saturn (Planet)—Juvenile literature.   [1. Saturn (Planet)]
I. Title.   II. Series: Vogt, Gregory. Gateway solar system.
QB671.V64   1993
523.4′6—dc20   92-30188   CIP   AC

Photographs and illustrations courtesy National Aeronautics
and Space Administration

Solar system diagram by Anne Canevari Green

SATURN

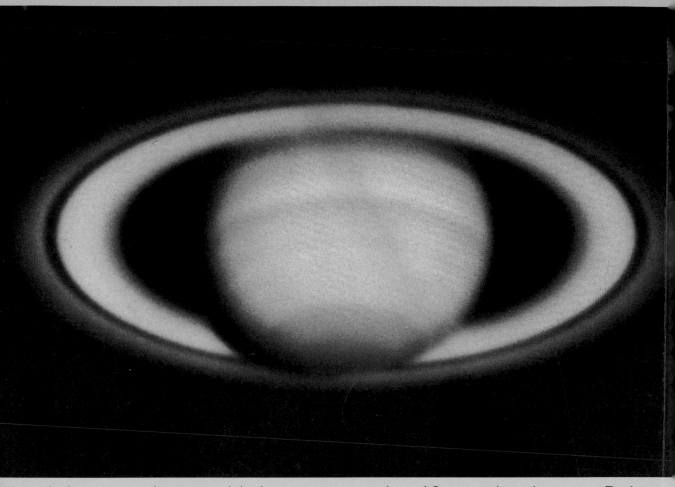

As fuzzy as it is, this is one of the best pictures ever taken of Saturn with a telescope on Earth. The dark gap in the middle of the planet's rings is the Cassini Division.

One dark night in the year 1610, the Italian scientist Galileo Galilei pointed a simple telescope toward the planet Saturn. It was the very first time anyone had seen Saturn through a telescope.

The telescope's lenses were small. Galileo's view of Saturn was poor. All the same, Galileo made a startling discovery. Saturn was round, but it had two bumps on its sides!

Galileo called the bumps "ears." He did not live long enough to find out what they really were. A Dutch scientist, Christiaan Huygens, answered that question years later.

In 1656, Huygens used a bigger and better telescope to look at Saturn. He decided that Galileo's "ears" were really a solid ring surrounding the planet.

Astronomers—scientists who study objects in outer space—built still larger and better telescopes. And the view of Saturn became clearer and clearer. In 1675 a French astronomer, Jean Dominique Cassini, found a dark band running through the middle of Huygens's ring. The dark band was really a gap, dividing the ring in two. It was named the *Cassini Division,* after its discoverer.

Now Saturn was known to have two rings. And astronomers thought that the rings were probably not solid after all. Cassini also discovered four moons orbiting Saturn.

And so it went. With each improved telescope, astronomers saw Saturn more clearly and made new discoveries about this mysterious planet.

One of the most amazing things astronomers observed about Saturn's rings was that they sometimes disappeared! The disappearances were easy to explain once astronomers realized that the rings are very thin. At times, the rings were turned partly toward Earth. Then they formed an oval. But at other times, the thin edge of the rings faced Earth. Then the rings could not be seen at all.

To see this effect for yourself, ask a friend to hold up an old phonograph record or a compact disk at the end of a long hall. Stand at the other end and watch your friend slowly flip the disk over and over. The disk will seem to disappear when its edge is toward you.

Spacecraft Study Saturn

For hundreds of years, astronomers could learn about Saturn only by looking through telescopes. Because these telescopes were on Earth, their image of Saturn was al-

An artist's drawing of the *Pioneer 11* spacecraft passing Saturn.

ways blurred by air currents and haze in Earth's atmo-sphere.

Then, in the mid-1970s, three spacecraft were sent out into deep space by the National Aeronautics and Space Administration (NASA). The spacecraft flew first to Jupiter and then on to Saturn. The first to arrive at Saturn was *Pioneer 11*. It was followed a few years later by *Voyager 1* and *Voyager 2*. The spacecraft carried cameras, and they radioed pictures back to Earth.

The Hubble Space Telescope as it was placed in orbit from the space shuttle.

In 1990 another spacecraft was launched. But this one didn't fly to Saturn. It remained in Earth *orbit* (traveling around Earth) above the atmosphere. This was the Hubble Space Telescope (HST). It, too, has been used to study Saturn.

Each of NASA's spacecraft has helped us learn much about Saturn. And Saturn has turned out to be more exciting than any astronomer had dreamed. Before we look at what astronomers discovered, let's first review what we know about Saturn's place in the solar system.

The Sixth Planet

Saturn is the sixth planet out from the sun. It orbits the sun at a distance of 888 million miles (1,428 million kilometers). This is ten times farther away than Earth.

Being much farther away from the sun means that a Saturn year (one orbit) is much longer than an Earth year. It takes Saturn almost 30 Earth years to complete one orbit. Saturn is also much bigger than Earth. With a diameter of 74,899 miles (120,536 kilometers), it is the second-largest planet in our solar system. (Jupiter is the largest.)

Saturn is a giant ball of gas. The gas is mostly hydrogen and helium, with very small amounts of methane and ethane mixed in. The planet has no solid surface, but astronomers believe it has a rocky core.

Hydrogen and helium are both very lightweight gases. This makes Saturn very light for a planet its size. If you could place Saturn in a giant tub of water, the planet would float!

The gas in Saturn's upper atmosphere is very cold, almost 287 degrees below zero Fahrenheit (−177 degrees Celsius). Strong winds blow around the planet at speeds of up to 1,110 miles (1,800 kilometers) per hour.

Some of the clouds of Saturn are the color of but-

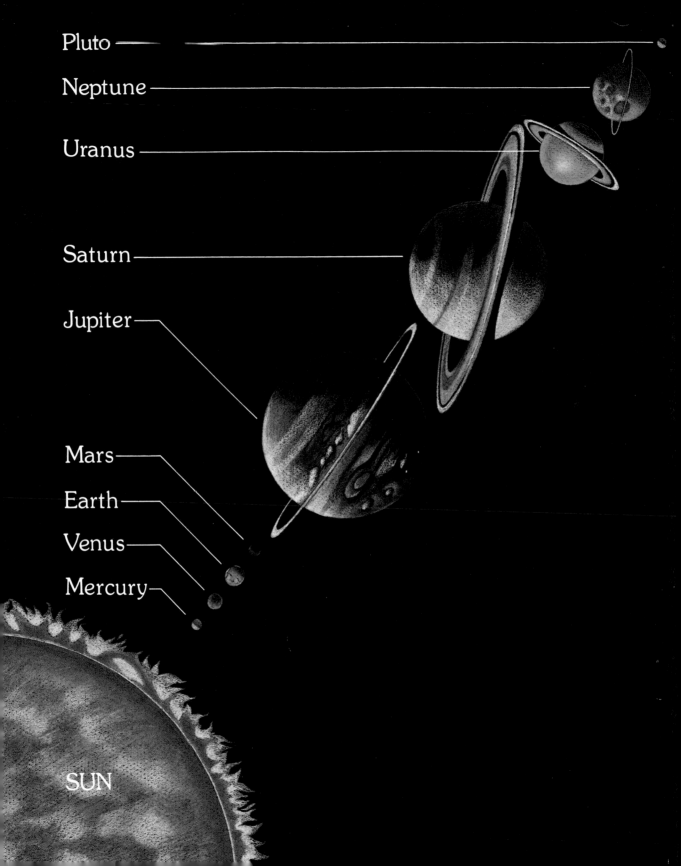

Pluto

Neptune

Uranus

Saturn

Jupiter

Mars

Earth

Venus

Mercury

SUN

Saturn as seen from *Voyager*. When the spacecraft took this picture, it was still too far away to see fine details in the planet's ring system.

terscotch. Between them, where we see deeper into darker regions, are what look like narrow *bands* circling the planet parallel to its *equator*. There are also dark, oval-shaped storms on the planet. But both the bands and ovals are hard to see because the highest part of Saturn's atmosphere is hazy.

By using computers to change and brighten colors, scientists are able to see more detail.

Sometimes the weather on Saturn changes. A short time after NASA's Hubble Space Telescope was launched, astronomers noticed that a huge white cloud was beginning to form over Saturn's equator. The HST was pointed toward the planet so that the cloud could be studied.

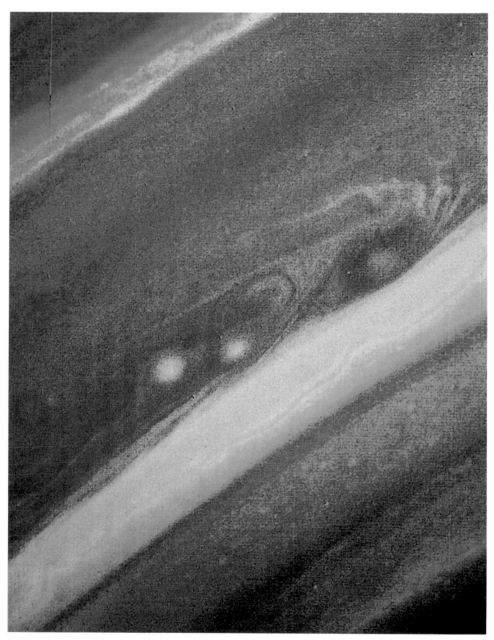

Bright spots, bands, and fast-moving clouds appear in this close-up of Saturn's atmosphere. The colors were changed to show greater detail.

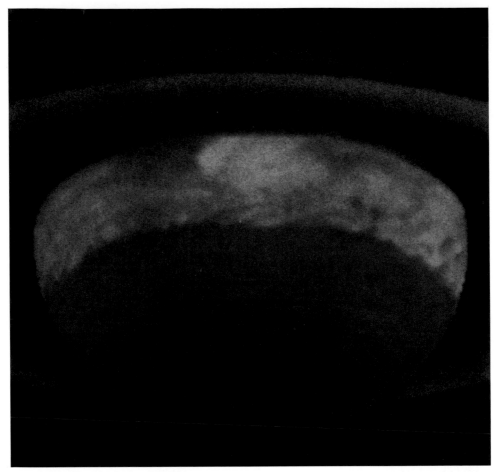

Pictures taken by the Hubble Space Telescope reveal a huge white cloud over the planet's midsection.

For several months, the cloud spread across the equator and rose higher and higher. Astronomers believe it to be made of ammonia ice crystals, but they don't know what caused it to form.

The Rings

Saturn's rings are very large and very thin. The inner edge of the rings starts 4,350 miles (7,000 kilometers) from Saturn's cloud tops. The outer edge that can be seen from Earth extends to 45,960 miles (74,000 kilometers) away. At most, the rings are only about 3 miles (5 kilometers) thick.

The *Pioneer 11* spacecraft provided a good view of Saturn's rings. It also found more rings, bringing the total of known rings to six. But when the *Voyagers* flew by, astronomers had an even clearer view. *Voyagers'* cameras were better than *Pioneer*'s, and they showed that the rings were made of many *ringlets*. As the *Voyagers* got closer and closer, the number of ringlets climbed to the dozens, then hundreds, and finally thousands! Seen from close up, Saturn's ringlets looked like the tiny grooves on a CD.

The ringlets are made up of many small particles, each orbiting Saturn like a tiny moon. The smallest particles are the size of a speck of dust, while the largest are as big as a house. Scientists believe the rings were created when one or more of Saturn's moons were struck by comets or asteroids and shattered. After the collisions, the fragments spread out around the planet in rings.

15

Saturn's ringlets are not perfect circles. Many ringlets have kinks in them. The kinks are caused by the *gravity,* or pull, of nearby moons. These moons act like "shepherds" to keep the ringlet particles in line. Sometimes the *shepherd moons,* moving in different orbits, are near each other. At other times they are far apart. Because of this, their gravitational pull plays tug-of-war on the ringlet particles. This bends or changes the shape of the ringlets.

When *Voyager* was still 5.5 million miles (8.9 million km) from Saturn, hundreds of ringlets became visible. The ringlets have been given special colors here, to make details easier to see.

Finer detail can be seen in close-up views of the ringlets.

Another interesting feature of Saturn's ringlets is that there are *spokes*. The spokes are dark shadows crossing many ringlets and pointing outward away from Saturn. They look like the spokes on a bicycle wheel but are fuzzy and not always visible.

Astronomers think the spokes may be made of very fine dust particles that are attracted by static electricity. (To see how static electricity attracts dust particles, lightly shake a dust rag near the screen of a television set that is turned on. The screen, charged with static electricity, attracts the dust particles.) The dust particles of Saturn's spokes seem to be floating above the rings, but astronomers aren't sure why they do this.

Saturn's Moons

When the *Voyager* spacecraft approached Saturn, astronomers knew the planet had ten moons, or *satellites*. (A satellite is a small body that orbits a larger body in space. Moons are "natural satellites" that orbit planets. Orbiting spacecraft are sometimes called "artificial satellites" because they are made by people.) By the time the spacecraft passed by the planet, seven new moons had been discovered.

Today, the official moon count is up to 18. But that number is likely to increase with new space missions to the planet. There are probably many small moons orbiting Saturn, waiting to be discovered.

Saturn's moons come in all shapes and sizes. Tiny potato-shaped Atlas is 19 miles long by 12 miles wide (30 by 19 kilometers). It is the second closest of Saturn's known satellites and orbits just 10,600 miles (17,066 kilometers) above the planet's clouds. Atlas and several other of Saturn's smallest moons are probably fragments of smashed larger moons.

Farthest out, about 8 million miles (almost 13 million kilometers) away, is Phoebe. Phoebe is about the size of the states of New Hampshire and Vermont combined. This moon is the oddball of the Saturn moon

Individual pictures taken by the *Voyager* spacecraft were combined to make this picture of Saturn and some of its moons. The faint lines across some of the planet's rings are the mysterious spokes discovered by *Voyager*.

system. It orbits the planet in the opposite direction from all the rest. Because of this, astronomers think Phoebe is not one of Saturn's natural moons. It is probably a stray asteroid that was captured into orbit by Saturn's gravitational pull.

One of Saturn's moons, Titan, is so large that it has its own atmosphere. For this to happen, a moon or a planet must have a strong gravitational field, to keep the gas from escaping into space. Titan has a diameter of 3,200 miles (5,150 kilometers). That's 200 miles (320 kilometers) bigger than the diameter of the planet Mercury!

Astronomers are very interested in Titan because of its unusual atmosphere. It is made of nitrogen and methane gases. The pressure of the thick layer of gases at Titan's surface is equal to what you would experience if you were diving under Earth's oceans at a depth of 16 feet (5 meters).

Titan is very cold. Instruments on the spacecraft that flew by Titan measured the moon's surface temperature at 290 degrees below zero Fahrenheit (−179 degrees Celsius). Despite the cold, chemical reactions occur in its atmosphere. These reactions form poisonous gases, such as ethane. Some of the gases become rain or snow that falls to the moon's surface. Some astronomers think Ti-

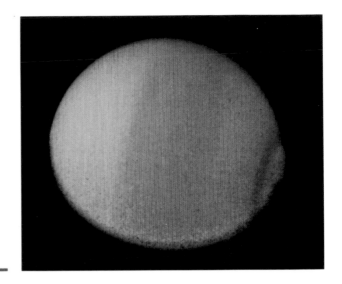

Because of Titan's hazy atmosphere, the surface of the moon cannot be seen in this picture.

tan may have lakes or oceans of liquid methane-ethane, with islands of water ice.

Another of Saturn's interesting moons is Enceladus. Enceladus appears to be made entirely of water ice, which gives this moon a very bright surface. The surface has cracks and valleys. This shows that Enceladus has a crust that moves as Earth's crust does.

Closer to Saturn than Enceladus is the rocky satellite Mimas. With a diameter of 244 miles (392 kilometers), Mimas is one of Saturn's smaller moons. But in spite of its small size, the moon is really remarkable. Mimas has a crater 81 miles (130 kilometers) in diameter smashed into its surface! The center of the crater has a mountain more than 6 miles (10 kilometers) jutting out

The surface of Saturn's moon Enceladus (left) shows cracks and valleys. The largest crater on Mimas (right) has a mountain in its center that is bigger than Mount Everest on Earth.

into space. The mountain is almost a mile higher than Mount Everest, the tallest mountain on Earth.

Sometime in Mimas's past, a large object, perhaps a *meteor,* struck this moon. The impact blasted out a big crater and created a lot of heat. The surface of Mimas melted in the heat and splashed about. It you throw a stone in a pond of water, you can see what must have happened next. When the stone hits the water, it makes a hole. Water rushes back to fill the hole and sloshes up in the middle.

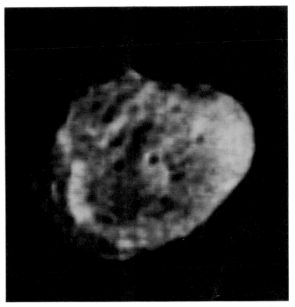

Half of the moon Iapetus (left) is light, and half is dark. Hyperion (right) is a bumpy, irregular-shaped satellite. Repeated meteor impacts have probably broken off large pieces of this moon.

The same thing happened where the meteor hit Mimas, but with one difference. Before the molten rock could settle down, it froze in the middle and formed a mountain.

Other strange moons orbit Saturn. Half of the moon Iapetus is dark in color, and half is light. Iapetus is made mainly of ice. Scientists think its dark side must have some impurities to give it the darker color.

Little Hyperion has taken a real beating. Its surface is full of meteor holes. Tethys has a giant valley system that stretches over nearly three fourths of its surface. The valley is many times larger than the Grand Canyon on Earth.

One of the great puzzles astronomers hope to solve someday is how life was created on Earth. Further study of Saturn and its moons may help astronomers answer this question.

Some astronomers think the atmosphere of Saturn's moon Titan may be similar to what Earth's atmosphere must have been like billions of years ago. Back then, there wasn't any life on Earth. If Titan's atmosphere is really like ancient Earth's atmosphere, then studying Titan's atmosphere would be like opening a history book of Earth.

This is exactly what astronomers hope to do when they send a new spacecraft to Saturn. The *Cassini Mission* will launch a two-part spacecraft to Saturn. An orbiter will circle the planet to study its rings and moons. A probe will parachute into the atmosphere of Titan and land on Titan's surface.

The Cassini Mission should answer many questions astronomers have about Saturn. But the discoveries it will make may lead to many more questions. Saturn holds enough mysteries to keep astronomers busy for centuries to come!

SATURN QUICK FACTS

Saturn: Named after the ancient Roman god of agriculture.

	Saturn	Earth
Average Distance From the Sun		
Millions of miles	888	93
Millions of kilometers	1,428	150
Revolution (one orbit around the sun)	29.46 years	1 year
Average Orbital Speed		
Miles per second	6	18.6
Kilometers per second	9.65	30
Rotation (spinning once)	10 hours, 40 minutes	24 hours
Diameter at Equator		
Miles	74,899	7,926
Kilometers	120,536	12,756
Surface Gravity (compared to Earth's)	1.08	1
Mass (the amount of matter contained in Saturn, compared to Earth)	95.18	1
Atmosphere	hydrogen, helium	nitrogen, oxygen
Satellites (moons)	18	1
Rings	thousands	0

Saturn's Moons	Diameter	Distance From Planet
1981S13	12 mi 20 km	83,005 mi 133,580 km
Atlas*	19 mi 30 km	85,546 mi 137,670 km
Prometheus*	62 mi 100 km	86,590 mi 139,350 km
Pandora*	56 mi 90 km	88,051 mi 141,700 km
Epimetheus*	75 mi 120 km	94,091 mi 151,420 km
Janus*	118 mi 190 km	94,122 mi 151,470 km
Mimas	244 mi 392 km	115,280 mi 185,520 km
Enceladus	311 mi 500 km	147,903 mi 238,020 km
Tethys	659 mi 1,060 km	183,061 mi 294,660 km
Telesto*	19 mi 30 km	183,061 km 294,660 km
Calypso*	16 mi 26 km	183,061 mi 294,660 km
Dione	696 mi 1,120 km	234,512 mi 377,400 km
Helene*	20 mi 32 km	234,512 mi 377,400 km
Rhea	951 mi 1,530 km	327,496 mi 527,040 km

Saturn's Moons	Diameter	Distance From Planet
Titan	3,200 mi	759,230 mi
	5,150 km	1,221,830 km
Hyperion *	180 mi	920,338 mi
	290 km	1,481,100 km
Iapetus	907 mi	2,212,950 mi
	1,460 km	3,561,300 km
Phoebe	137 mi	8,048,220 mi
	220 km	12,952,000 km

*These moons are not round. The longest dimension is given.

GLOSSARY

Astronomer	A scientist who studies planets, moons, stars, and other objects in outer space.
Band	A dark cloud that circles Saturn parallel to its equator.
Cassini Division	A dark region that appears to separate Saturn's rings when the rings are observed from a great distance.
Cassini Mission	A planned new space mission to Saturn.
Equator	An imaginary line running around the middle of a planet and halfway between the planet's north and south poles.
Gravity	A force that causes all objects to attract each other.
Hubble Space Telescope	The orbiting observatory launched by NASA in 1990.
Mass	The amount of matter contained in an object.
Meteor	A piece of space rock that shoots through space and creates a crater when it crashes into a planet or moon.
Orbit	The path a planet takes to travel around the sun, or a moon or a spacecraft to travel around a planet.
Pioneer 11	Spacecraft that visited Jupiter in the mid-1970s and then flew by Saturn in the late 1970s.
Revolution	One complete orbit of a planet around the sun, or a moon around a planet.
Ringlets	The name given to the thousands of individual rings circling Saturn.

Rotation	The spinning of a planet or moon around its axis (an imaginary line through the center of the planet, from the north pole to the south pole).
Satellite	A small body in space that orbits around a larger body. A satellite may be "natural," as a moon, or "artificial," as a spacecraft.
Shepherd moons	Moons orbiting near Saturn that help some ringlets maintain their circular shape.
Spokes	Shadowy, spokelike dark lines crossing Saturn's ringlets.
Voyager 1 and *2*	Spacecraft that visited Jupiter in the late 1970s and then flew by Saturn in the early 1980s.

FOR FURTHER READING

Asimov, I. *Saturn: The Ringed Beauty.* Milwaukee: Gareth Stevens, 1988.

Gallant, R. *The Planets, Exploring the Solar System.* New York: Four Winds Press, 1982.

Landau, E. *Saturn.* New York: Franklin Watts, 1991.

Simon, S. *Saturn.* New York: William Morrow, 1985.

Vogt, G. *Voyager.* Brookfield, Conn.: The Millbrook Press, 1991.

INDEX

ABOUT THE AUTHOR

Gregory L. Vogt works for NASA's Education Division at the Johnson Space Center in Houston, Texas. He works with astronauts in developing educational videos for schools.

Mr. Vogt previously served as executive director of the Discovery World Museum of Science, Economics and Technology in Milwaukee, Wisconsin, and as an eighth grade science teacher. He holds bachelor's and master's degrees in science from the University of Wisconsin at Milwaukee, as well as a doctorate in curriculum and instruction from Oklahoma State University.